INTRODUCTION

In an age of rapid technological advancements, increasing expectations, and unparalleled professional competition, the challenges and pressures of the modern workplace have become greater than ever. Individuals constantly grapple with staying focused, managing stress, and maintaining personal happiness as they forge ahead in their careers. With the stakes so high, finding the key to professional growth and stability has never been more vital. It might seem surprising, then, that one of the most powerful answers to these pressing issues can be found in an ancient philosophy that has much to teach us despite being over two thousand years old —stoicism.

"Unwavering Success: Harnessing Stoic Wisdom to Revolutionize Your Work Life" delves into the ageless philosophy of stoicism, exploring its relevance, significance, and practical applications in today's ever-evolving workplace. The purpose of this book is to provide readers with the knowledge and tools necessary to harness stoic wisdom, empowering them to create a fulfilling, thriving work life. By embracing stoic principles, individuals can navigate the modern workplace with poise, resilience, and an inner strength that fosters happiness, success, and personal growth.

The stoic philosophy has long been appreciated for its timeless lessons that empower one to rise above the chaos of everyday life by cultivating mental toughness, emotional intelligence, and a strong sense of personal ethics. Despite the vast transformations in our world since the time of the ancient stoics, the teachings of Epictetus, Seneca, and Marcus Aurelius continue to resonate profoundly with those who have discovered the immense value in their wisdom.

Traditionally, stoicism has been a champion of cultivating a steadfast character and rational mindset, which are essential for succeeding in any profession. This book is intended to be an invaluable resource for those who seek to advance their that can be seamlessly integrated into work life. By uncovering the essence of stoicism and its teachings, working professionals can adopt easily implementable strategies that will measurably impact their workplace performance.

Throughout this book, you will be introduced to tried and tested concepts, including principles like the Dichotomy of Control, which offers actionable guidance on how to focus on factors within one's control rather than dwelling on external circumstances. Along the journey, you will also encounter compelling anecdotes drawn from historic stoic figures and real-life professionals that showcase the impact of stoicism in diverse situations.

Moreover, "Unwavering Success" provides readers with a framework designed to foster exceptional leadership to become an indispensable asset for any organization. Drawing upon the wisdom of stoic leaders from the past, this book presents guidance on how to cultivate emotional intelligence, empathy, and adaptability that will have a lasting positive impact on both personal growth and one's professional environment.

UNWAVERING SUCCESS

Harnessing Stoic Wisdom to Revolutionize Your Work Life

ALEXANDRA K PARKER

In addition to leadership, the book delves into other essential aspects of work life—collaboration and teamwork. By exploring the central role that stoic principles play in building healthy, supportive, and efficient teams, readers will discover how communication and camaraderie can directly contribute to success. "Unwavering Success" ensures that you are equipped with the necessary knowledge to leverage stoicism's power to advance team cohesion and grow in tandem with your colleagues.

Furthermore, this book acknowledges the importance of achieving a harmonious balance between work life and personal life. Discover how stoicism can help you navigate the delicate interplay between these two spheres, ensuring a sense of fulfillment both in your career and your personal endeavors. By finding guidance through the stoic philosophy, you'll take steps towards a more focused, contented, and ethically-grounded life.

"Unwavering Success: Harnessing Stoic Wisdom to Revolutionize Your Work Life" strives to illuminate the power of stoicism to transform not only individual lives but also entire organizations. As you progress through each chapter, you will be provided with practical steps to implement stoic principles at an organizational level, paving the way for more ethical, innovative, and productive work cultures.

By connecting the ageless wisdom of stoicism to present-day challenges, this book offers an indispensable resource for those seeking to revolutionize their work life. As you embark on this journey through the pages of "Unwavering Success," prepare to unlock the profound power that lies within stoicism—a philosophy that has seen the test of time and continues to resonate with those who dare to embrace its lessons.

As you delve into the timeless teachings of stoicism and explore their applications in your professional world, "Unwavering Success" aims to inspire, educate, and empower. May the pages of this book become a steadfast companion on your journey to unlocking the immense potential that resides within you and mastering the modern workplace with unwavering strength, tenacity, and wisdom.

Chapter One

THE ART OF STOIC ADAPTABILITY: THRIVING IN A CONSTANTLY EVOLVING WORKPLACE

In today's rapidly changing professional landscape, uncertainty and constant evolution seem to be the only guarantees. To succeed in this environment, workers are increasingly seeking models of adaptability that can empower them to flourish despite challenges. In the realm of philosophy, Stoicism has emerged as a uniquely practical and time-tested approach to not only surviving but actually thriving under such conditions.

Stoicism, an ancient Greek and Roman philosophy, encourages the development of self-control and endurance, traits that are vital in our modern workplaces. At its core, Stoicism is about understanding and cultivating personal virtues like wisdom, courage, temperance, and justice. Based on a keen awareness of the impermanence of the world and the idea that the only real control we have is over our own thoughts and actions, Stoicism offers a powerful toolkit to meet the demands of the contemporary professional environment.

. . .

In this chapter, we will explore the origins and key teachings of Stoicism and explain why the principles behind this ancient philosophy remain incredibly relevant and useful today. By embracing Stoicism, you will be prepared to navigate the complexities and uncertainties of the professional world with confidence, resilience, and adaptability.

UNRAVELING THE PHILOSOPHY

The birth of Stoicism can be traced back to Athens in the 3rd century BCE. Founded by Zeno of Citium, an ancient Greek philosopher, the school of Stoicism derived its name from the Stoa Poikile, the Athenian gathering place where Zeno and his students would teach and discuss their ideas. Stoicism grew in prominence, becoming one of the foremost philosophies of the Hellenistic era and later spreading throughout the Roman Empire. Among the most renowned Stoics are Seneca, Epictetus, and the Roman Emperor Marcus Aurelius.

These thinkers recognized the value of developing an inner wisdom and personal fortitude to weather the storms of life. They believed that, despite the chaos and unpredictability of the world, serenity and purpose could be found in leading a life guided by reason and virtue. By prioritizing personal development and ethical decision-making, Stoics sought to cultivate a stable and resilient sense of self, able to withstand the vicissitudes of fortune.

The central teaching of Stoicism is the dichotomy of control, which states that some things are within our control, and some things are not. This seemingly simple insight has profound implications. By recognizing and focusing on what we can control—our thoughts, actions, and reactions—Stoics maintain that we can achieve a state of tranquility and happiness, regardless of external circumstances. At the same time, the Stoics emphasized that it is essential to practice wisdom in distinguishing between what is within our control and what is not, thereby avoiding unnecessary suffering caused by unfulfillable desires or unrealistic expectations.

NAVIGATING MODERN WORKPLACES WITH STOIC WISDOM

Why has this ancient philosophical school kept its relevance in the ultra-modern world? A major contributing factor is the universality of the obstacles Stoics sought to overcome. In both our personal lives and careers, we are still confronted with capricious fortune and confounding dilemmas, making the Stoic goal of inner strength and tranquility as appealing now as ever.

In a time when the world is continuously transformed by technology, globalization, and social shifts, the ability to adapt to change is of paramount importance. This is particularly true in the workplace, which is often marked by uncertainty, turbulence, and insecurity. Many of us have experienced or know someone who has encountered a sudden job loss, a sudden shift in a company's direction, or the need to learn new skills quickly to avoid obsolescence. And this is not to mention the day-to-day challenges that can cause stress and frustration, such as demanding deadlines, uncooperative colleagues, and unanticipated roadblocks.

. . .

It's in such circumstances that an adaptive, resourceful mindset becomes essential. By adopting the Stoic determination to control only what is within our power and to let go of what is not, we immediately become more decisive, resilient, and effective in both our professional and personal lives. By focusing our energy solely on the aspects of the world we can influence, we become more productive, resourceful, and nimble in the face of change.

Take the example of Marcus Aurelius, the last of the "Five Good Emperors" and one of the most thoughtful and enlightened rulers in Roman history. In his Meditations, a series of intimate reflections and admonishments to himself, Marcus confronts the challenges of power, warfare, and court politics with measured and deliberate self-reflection. Rather than being rendered paralyzed or reactive by events beyond his control, Marcus maintains a clear-eyed focus on his duties and responsibilities, guided always by reason and virtue.

By approaching the inherently uncertain terrain of the modern workplace with a similar Stoic disposition, we are better able to maintain our focus, minimize anxiety, and make clear-headed and well-reasoned decisions. Thus, an adaptable Stoic mindset is indispensable in our professional endeavors.

AN INTRODUCTION TO STOIC TECHNIQUES

Now that we've explored the origins and key teachings of Stoicism, let's delve into some of the specific techniques that can be employed to foster resilience, adaptability, and contentment in the modern workplace. While the heart of the Stoic practice lies in recognizing the dichotomy of control, several complementary techniques refine and enrich this insight.

One foundational Stoic practice is the concept of premeditatio malorum, or premeditating adversity. This practice entails visualizing potential challenges, setbacks, and obstacles that we may encounter in our lives, in order to prepare our minds for dealing with them effectively. By imagining ourselves successfully overcoming these challenges, we are mentally rehearsing the skills, virtues, and mindset required to handle them with grace, wisdom, and courage. In a professional setting, this can be applied by regularly considering and planning for possible career obstacles, changes in the industry or organizational structure, and even potential personal setbacks.

Another essential Stoic technique is the practice of amor fati, or the "love of fate." Stoics embrace the belief that everything that occurs is an integral part of the universal web of events and has a purpose within the greater whole, even if we may not always understand it. Thus, rather than bemoaning our misfortune or dwelling on complaints, Stoics strive to see the good in every situation and to grow from every experience, remaining adaptable and focused on the things within their control. This concept is especially valuable in the workplace since it guides us beyond the urge to rail against circumstances and steers us toward constructive problem-solving and adaptation.

As we work through the following chapters, we will further examine these techniques and many others, investigating how they can be applied in real-world situations to improve our work lives.

By reintroducing the Stoic principles and techniques discussed in this chapter to our daily lives, we lay the groundwork for a more adaptable, resilient, and purpose-driven approach to navigating the complexities of the modern workplace. As we move forward in this exploration, in subsequent chapters, we will delve deeper into specific Stoic insights and explore their applications to workplace relationships, leadership, teamwork, and personal well-being.

In the whirlwind of our professional lives, we can learn from the Stoics the art of staying grounded, centered, and continually ready to learn and grow. As we embrace the Stoic path, we step confidently into the ever-changing landscape of the workplace, armed with a philosophy that empowers us to thrive in the midst of unsuspected challenges, inevitable setbacks, and unforeseeable opportunities.

Chapter Two

MASTERING EMOTIONS: CULTIVATING A POWERFUL MENTAL FRAMEWORK

The modern workplace is a complex and demanding environment that creates myriad opportunities for stress and emotional volatility. Workers in every field grapple with long hours, competing demands on their time and attention, and the ever-looming pressure to meet increasingly challenging goals. In this high-tension atmosphere, learning how to control one's emotions and maintain focus is the key to not only personal resilience but also professional success. This is where the ancient mental discipline of stoicism can be a tremendous asset to modern workers. By applying the core principles of stoic philosophy, individuals can master their emotions, stay present in the face of obstacles, and unlock a newfound level of productivity and creativity.

Let us begin with an exploration of the dichotomy of control, which is central to understanding the necessity of emotional mastery in the contemporary workplace. This fundamental stoic idea posits that there are things in life we have direct control over, and others we do not. We can influence our thoughts, opinions, beliefs, and reactions, but external events and how others respond are outside our scope of influence.

Given this distinction, stoics argue that it is both rational and adaptive to focus our energies and emotional investments on those aspects of life within our control, and accept those outside it with serenity. When applied to the workplace, this principle underscores the importance of focusing on our tasks, personal improvement, and responses to challenges, instead of dwelling on the whims of a volatile market or the endless sea of office politics.

This simple but profound notion of dichotomy of control can be transformative in the way we approach our work. It allows us to remain composed and undeterred amid hardships, such as sudden project setbacks, uncooperative teammates, or unattainable deadlines. By concentrating on our locus of control, we can more effectively manage the emotional turbulence that often derails us in high-pressure situations.

Yet cultivating emotional mastery does not occur overnight. It requires regular practice using a range of cognitive techniques developed by stoic philosophers. These techniques can be utilized in diverse settings, from your daily commute to your workplace or during times of personal reflection.

Take, for example, the case of Jared, a manager at a multinational corporation. Jared was overwhelmed by the stress of balancing the numerous pressing demands placed on him: achieving ambitious sales targets, managing his team effectively, and maintaining his work-life balance. Feeling trapped in a cycle of anxiety and worry, Jared turned to stoicism for guidance.

He began the practice of premeditatio malorum, or premeditation of evils. This technique involves deliberately envisioning worst-case scenarios and considering how to meet those challenges or accept their consequences with equanimity. By regularly exposing himself to the imagined pain and turmoil of potential failure, Jared began to build his mental resilience.

Over time, he learned that the fear of these grim outcomes was far worse than their reality. In doing so, Jared honed his ability to stay focused and calm, even when confronted with the most trying circumstances. His newfound stoic mindset helped him emerge from his cocoon of fear and anxiety, propelling him forward to a more balanced and fulfilling work life.

Another powerful cognitive technique for mastering emotions is the practice of self-distancing. By stepping outside oneself and adopting an objective perspective, it becomes easier to untangle the webs of irrational thought and emotion that often ensnare our minds.

Imagine facing a challenging project at work that threatens to cripple your confidence. While it might be tempting to let your emotions take over and descend into a spiral of self-doubt, stoicism suggests a healthier approach. Visualize yourself from the vantage point of an impartial observer, examining the situation as if analyzing it for a friend or colleague. This self-distancing technique affords you the clarity to evaluate the situation more dispassionately, which can lead to more productive and solutions-oriented thinking.

It is essential, however, not to mistake this stoic practice for repression or avoidance of feelings. A pivotal aspect of stoicism is self-awareness and emotional honesty. While the goal is to manage your emotions effectively, acknowledging their existence is imperative. Allowing yourself to feel, and then choosing to shift focus or reframe a situation, is a healthier and more sustainable route to emotional mastery.

To further illustrate this concept, let us consider the experiences of Laura, a journalist navigating a highly competitive and unpredictable work environment. Tasked with covering high-profile news events, Laura struggled to maintain her composure in the face of tight deadlines, sensational stories, and a highly critical audience. Consumed by her emotions and plagued by bouts of self-doubt, Laura realized she needed a change.

Inspired by stoic philosophy, she began exploring strategies for managing her emotions more effectively. Laura started by acknowledging her fear of failure and the pressure she was feeling. Then, using the stoic principle of turning obstacles into opportunities, she reframed her struggles as chances for growth.

This seemingly simple but powerful mental shift enabled Laura to meet challenges head-on, swifter in her work and more adaptive in her approach. Her confidence soared, and subsequently, her work flourished. To this day, Laura looks back on her days of emotional turmoil as a critical turning point in her journalistic career.

The transformative power of stoicism is evident in the real-life examples of Jared and Laura. By understanding and applying the core principles of this ancient philosophy, they each crafted mental frameworks better equipped to handle the stress and pressure of the modern workplace. The stoic ability to master one's emotions not only allowed them to thrive within their respective fields but also created a foundation for lasting personal and professional fulfillment.

As you embark on your journey to emotional mastery through the wisdom of stoicism, remember that change is a gradual process. Dedication, patience, and self-compassion are necessary tools in fully integrating these concepts into your everyday life. In time, you will find yourself better able to navigate the complex emotional terrain of the workplace, empowered by an unshakable mental framework and an unwavering will to succeed.

Chapter Three

THE STOIC LEADER - INSPIRING GROWTH AND INNOVATION IN THE WORKPLACE

Throughout history, stoicism has provided moral and intellectual guidance to individuals seeking wisdom and stability amid life's challenges. In the workplace, the principles of stoicism can serve not only as a grounding philosophy but also as a powerful framework for effective leadership. The Stoic Leader inspires trust, respect, and commitment in those around them, unlocking the potential for growth and innovation across the organization.

One of the greatest assets of a stoic leader is their unwavering commitment to the principles of stoicism. They maintain a cool head under pressure and exude an air of composure that calms and inspires their team. Simultaneously, stoic leaders possess the ability to listen attentively, ensuring that each member's voice is heard and respected. In this chapter, we will explore the core traits of a stoic leader and how applying these values can redefine leadership in the modern workplace. Through real-life examples and historical figures, we will journey toward discovering the true power of stoic leadership.

A notable antecedent for the stoic leader can be found in the figure of Marcus Aurelius, Roman emperor, and philosopher. Known as the "philosopher king," Aurelius dedicated himself to the study and practice of stoicism, applying its principles to the governance of a vast and diverse empire. He was both revered for his wisdom and trusted for his commitment to the ethical guidance of his rule. Aurelius' example demonstrates the importance of using one's moral compass to remain steadfast through turbulent times. Today's workplace may not hold the same challenges faced by an ancient emperor, but the need for ethical, compassionate, and decisive leadership remains the same.

In this light, stoicism promotes a balanced approach to work, which benefits not only the leader but those under their guidance. As stoic leaders navigate uncertain and ever-changing work landscapes, their ability to focus on what they can control – their mindset and response to challenges – serves as a powerful example to those around them. The element of emotional intelligence, or the capacity to navigate one's emotions and the emotions of others effectively, plays an essential role in this process, with the stoic leader showing empathy towards the varying emotions of their team members. By understanding the emotions and experiences of individuals in the workplace, leaders are better equipped to foster a supportive and productive environment.

. . .

Leadership, as viewed from the stoic perspective, is not merely about managing resources or overseeing their team's daily work. Instead, it's also about cultivating talent and fostering personal growth. This growth-oriented mindset emerges from the stoic principle of continual self-improvement. When a leader can recognize the potential for development and drives their team to seek out opportunities for exploration and expansion, it creates an environment where innovation can thrive. In return, the team members gain a sense of alignment with the organization's goals, feeling valued and motivated to contribute meaningfully.

History has bestowed us with myriad examples of stoic leaders influencing and shaping the development of their respective societies. For instance, George Washington, the first president of the United States, was heavily influenced by stoicism throughout his life, which echoes itself in his leadership as a general and a president. Washington exemplified key stoic virtues, such as wisdom, courage, justice, and moderation, which won him the trust and loyalty of those under his command. By putting these virtues into practice and exhibiting a steady temperament, he gained his army's faith and formed a stable government that could weather internal and external conflicts.

The decisiveness that is a hallmark of stoic leadership emerges from the ability to identify and weigh multiple competing interests while seeking the course of action most aligned with one's values and the overall good. This involves pragmatism and patience, as well as emotional detachment. It's essential, however, not to view emotional detachment as coldness or indifference, but rather as the capacity to take a step back, assess the situation objectively, and choose the most appropriate response.

Chapter Four

STRENGTHENING COLLABORATION: BUILDING BRIDGES THROUGH STOIC WISDOM

In a bustling office or virtual workplace, collective decision-making and collaborative work make up the bedrock of any thriving organization. Healthy team dynamics can lead to more engaging conversations, innovative solutions, and a sense of unity. However, friction within the team, communication breakdowns, or conflicts can hinder progress and disrupt the harmony of the workplace. The ancient philosophy of Stoicism offers a blueprint for promoting trust, efficiency, and optimal communication in the heart of the modern office.

One may wonder how an ancient school of thought, born from philosophers like Epictetus, Seneca, and Marcus Aurelius, can apply to our diverse, interconnected work environment. Stoicism provides timeless principles that are more relevant than ever in navigating the challenges and intricacies of workplace dynamics. The essence of Stoicism lies in maintaining tranquility, practicing self-control, and focusing on personal growth in all aspects of life. When applied to teamwork, these principles forge stronger, more cohesive teams that foster a sense of belonging and mutual understanding among its members.

EMPATHY AS A GUIDING PRINCIPLE

The foundation of successful teamwork begins with empathy - the ability to understand and share the feelings of others. Empathy in the workplace enables employees to see issues and projects from the perspective of their colleagues, encouraging a cooperative environment. Within the stoic principles, we can find a deep emphasis on empathy and understanding. Marcus Aurelius, the Roman Emperor, and Stoic philosopher once said, "Whenever you are about to find fault with someone, ask yourself the following question: What fault of mine most nearly resembles the one I am about to criticize?"

This quote exemplifies the Stoic practice of self-reflection when dealing with others. By examining our own imperfections and placing ourselves in our colleagues' shoes, we cultivate empathy and nurture productive relationships within the team. Embracing this mindset facilitates healthier connections and encourages individuals to work together more effectively.

Consider a scenario where a new team member joins a long-established group, and they struggle to adapt to the team's work processes. Without empathy, the team would likely become frustrated with the newcomer, leading to undue pressure on them and dissatisfaction within the team. Embracing empathy, the team could instead recognize the challenges faced by the newcomer and make an effort to support and mentor them. This approach fosters a supportive and inclusive atmosphere, where the new member can learn, adapt, and ultimately contribute to the team's success.

CONFLICT RESOLUTION THROUGH STOIC WISDOM

As much as we strive for a smooth-sailing ship, workplace conflicts are inevitable. Disagreements and disputes can occur for numerous reasons, be it miscommunications, clashing personalities, or diverging opinions on a project. However, Stoicism equips us with the tools to deal with these conflicts in a constructive manner.

Epictetus, one of the prominent Stoic thinkers, suggested that it is not external events that create distress, but our reaction to those events. By managing our thoughts and reactions with self-control, we can navigate even the most difficult conflict situations productively. With a calm demeanor and rational thinking, we foster an environment where disagreements are resolved without having lasting negative impacts on the team's productivity and harmony.

When conflicts arise, it is important for team members to adhere to the stoic principle of focusing on what is within their control. Understanding that we cannot control the actions or opinions of others helps us to look inward and focus on what we can change. Through self-reflection and open communication, teams can quickly identify the root cause of the problem, find a solution, and move forward without letting the conflict impede progress.

SHARED SUCCESS AND SUPPORT

A natural byproduct of practicing Stoicism in the workplace is developing an environment of shared success and support. The Stoic teachings value virtues such as wisdom, courage, and justice. Applying these virtues collectively creates a workplace culture where achieving collective success takes precedence over individual accomplishments. By eradicating an atmosphere driven by competition, team members are more inclined to help and mentor one another, leading to a more satisfying, productive, and thriving work environment.

When every team member views success as a mutual endeavor, it encourages a genuine spirit of cooperation among colleagues. This mindset reduces the likelihood of unhealthy competition, which can lead to rifts or information hoarding, and fosters a supportive environment where everyone is pulling together to achieve common goals.

CASE STUDIES OF COHESIVE TEAMS

The impact of embracing stoic principles within a work environment cannot be understated, and real-world examples can attest to this. Diving into the successes of cohesive teams driven by empathy, self-reflection, and shared accomplishments reveal the transformative nature of Stoicism in the workplace. While Stoicism does not necessarily create a magic formula that resolves all issues, it certainly provides the compass needed for navigating the complexities of team dynamics.

. . .

One particular case exemplifies the impact of Stoic principles on a struggling team. A software development team had been facing persistent issues with communication, missed deadlines, and a stressful work culture. The manager, inspired by Stoicism, decided to introduce the concepts of empathy and self-reflection to the team. They organized workshops and group discussions to redefine the team's values and focus on collective growth.

Over time, team members began to understand the value of self-reflection and empathy. Instead of finger-pointing, they shifted focus to identifying areas of improvement and working together to develop solutions. Soon, communication barriers dissolved, the team's harmony improved, and they delivered projects in a more timely and efficient manner. The change was palpable not only to the internal stakeholders but also to their clients, who lauded the team for their improved performance and demeanor.

CONCLUSION

The Stoic framework and principles, drawn from philosophers Epictetus, Seneca, and Marcus Aurelius, offer an elegant and constructive way to address the interpersonal and communicative challenges that inevitably arise in the workplace. Integrating empathy, self-reflection, and collaboration into our daily work life can transform a team into a cohesive, supportive, and successful unit.

When we adopt Stoicism as a guiding force in our teams, we create an environment where every colleague feels valued and understood. This framework, which advocates for emotional intelligence, open communication, and putting the team's interests first, enables individuals to grow personally and professionally.

The essence of Stoicism, characterized by tranquility, wisdom, and self-improvement, extends far beyond the walls of the ancient philosophy school. Its timeless principles have the power to revolutionize our work environment and cultivate productive, satisfied teams that drive organizations toward excellence. By fostering empathy, camaraderie, and tireless cooperative spirit, Stoicism can empower individuals and teams to achieve the pinnacle of success, the kind of success that is felt not just in the tangible accomplishments, but in the fulfillment and personal growth of every team member involved.

Chapter Five

A VISION FOR THE STOIC WORKPLACE: UNLOCKING THE POTENTIAL OF EVERY EMPLOYEE

In the previous chapters, we traversed the exciting and transformative world of stoicism as applied to various aspects of our work lives. We've seen how stoicism can help us create powerful mental frameworks, shape inspiring leadership, and foster meaningful collaboration. In this culminating chapter, we embrace the potential of extending the principles of stoicism across the organizational landscape.

The question remains: What would a workplace built upon the foundation of stoic principles look like? How would employees and teams thrive under this philosophy? How can organizations cultivate a culture that is both resilient and adaptable?

As we explore the possibilities of the stoic workplace, we will uncover the benefits of integrating stoicism at an organizational level. Such a work environment encourages innovation, resiliency, and a supportive culture, unlocking each employee's full potential. The time is ripe for envisioning the future and taking actionable steps to bring stoic principles to every layer of our professional lives.

A FRAMEWORK FOR SUCCESS

Imagine a work environment where employees enter each day equipped to tackle any challenge or obstacle that comes their way. This adaptable resilience is a collective reflection of the organization's core values and beliefs. Companies built upon the framework of stoic principles harness the emotional intelligence and mental fortitude developed by each employee.

In a stoic workplace, employees view change as an opportunity for growth rather than a reason for distress. Embracing the unknown, they find innovative ways to tackle emerging challenges, bolstered by the Dichotomy of Control. Companies that build their foundation on stoic ideas foster spaces where employees take ownership of their actions and thoughts, creating fertile ground for productivity and sound decision-making.

By weaving the virtues of wisdom, courage, justice, and temperance into the organizational fabric, companies operating on the stoic blueprint cultivate an ethical and supportive work culture. A sense of responsibility and integrity becomes the hallmark of every decision made within the organization. Every employee understands that they have the power to control their thoughts and actions, contributing to a communal sense of accountability.

ETHICAL DECISION-MAKING

A major challenge faced by many modern organizations is navigating ethical dilemmas that arise in an increasingly complex world. Whether it's determining the rights to data privacy, addressing potential conflicts of interest, or dealing with evolving ethical concerns, businesses need a strong moral compass to guide them through the murky waters of corporate morality.

Companies can look to stoicism as their north star. In a workplace where stoicism is deeply rooted, employees are encouraged to approach ethical dilemmas with the Four Virtues in mind: wisdom, courage, justice, and temperance. This steadfast moral compass will guide employees as they navigate complex work situations that require impartiality, fairness, and integrity.

For example, faced with the challenge of downsizing or layoffs, a stoic organization would prioritize justice and fairness. Managers and leaders would weigh the merits of different departments and job functions, taking appropriate measures to communicate with transparency, openly acknowledging the reasons behind the decision, and offering support to affected employees.

Similarly, when considering a business opportunity that could yield significant profit but involve morally dubious practices, the organization would return to its stoic roots. Choosing wisdom and justice over a blind pursuit of wealth, the stoic workplace demonstrates an unwavering commitment to ethical principles, even when faced with tempting opportunities.

FOCUSED GROWTH AND ADAPTATION

An organization embracing stoicism would thrive in an ever-changing, fast-paced world. Recognizing that growth, both professional and personal, is the cornerstone of adaptability, such a workplace would place this pursuit at the heart of its mission.

Focused growth involves a constant exercise of self-examination and reflection, as well as a willingness to learn from challenges and successes alike. Within a stoic organization, employees are trained to approach each experience as a lesson, with an eagerness to extract maximum insight from every situation.

Managers lead by example, investing in their professional development, and constantly refining their skill set, all while embracing the principles of continuous improvement. They recognize that developing their abilities ultimately benefits the entire organization by setting a standard for growth and adaptability.

This focus also extends to how the organization performs its core functions. In a stoic workplace, practices are assessed and revised regularly, ensuring that the company adapts to the ever-changing landscape of the business world. Employees learn to pivot and respond to challenges, embracing new methodologies and tools at an agile pace.

PROMOTING COLLABORATION

The stoic workplace breeds a culture that values collaboration and the pursuit of shared success. Recognizing that we
are interconnected at every level, employees within stoic
organizations work together to achieve common goals.

Teams built on a stoic foundation foster environments where
open communication, constructive feedback, and mutual
support feature as indispensable elements. This collaboration
first shines through in how tasks are assigned and projects are
managed. The stoic manager understands the strengths and
weaknesses of each team member, channeling their collective
energy towards reaching goals efficiently.

Regular check-ins within the team ensure that employees feel
heard and valued. Concerns are met with empathy and understanding, fortifying the strength of interpersonal relationships. The stoic leader recognizes that emotional intelligence
is a vital asset; they encourage employees to sharpen those
skills, leading to improved teamwork, trust, and camaraderie.

The stoic workplace thrives by placing value in compassion
and cooperation. Managers and employees embrace the idea
of shared growth, working together to uncover innovative
solutions, navigate obstacles, and redefine the limits of their
potential.

ACHIEVING THE VISION

The vision of a stoic workplace may seem tantalizingly close, yet one must consider the challenging journey to get there. By taking actionable steps, organizations can foster communities where stoic principles provide a sustainable foundation on which employees can flourish.

1. Leadership buy-in: It is crucial that company leaders understand and support the notion of a stoic workplace. This not only ensures allocation of resources towards formalizing these practices but also inspires employees when they see stoic values reflected in their management.

2. Training and development: Develop customized workshops, seminars, and training courses that introduce the concepts of stoicism to employees at every level. Create opportunities for employees to learn through case studies, role-playing, and interactive challenges.

3. Integration of stoic principles into company culture: Reinforce stoic values by integrating them into the company's mission and vision statements. Reference these principles during critical decision-making processes, ensuring that they genuinely manifest in daily practices.

4. Encourage mindfulness practices: Develop company-wide programs that promote mindfulness, meditation, and reflection, supporting employees in adopting stoic practices through their everyday lives.

. . .

5. Celebrate stoic successes: Cite examples of successful organizational and individual outcomes due to the adoption of stoic principles, reinforcing the significance and potential of a stoic workplace.

The future of the stoic workplace is one of boundless potential. By embracing these ancient principles as pillars for modern organizational excellence, employees and businesses stand poised to excel in a fast-changing world. The time has come for our stoic journey to enter the realms of reality, where we shall unlock the full potential of every employee, guided by the unwavering wisdom of stoicism.

FINAL THOUGHTS

In the journey we have undertaken across the pages of "Unwavering Success: Harnessing Stoic Wisdom to Revolutionize Your Work Life," we have sought to illuminate the transformative strength and significance of stoicism in today's fast-paced, ever-evolving work environment. From building resilience to fostering team dynamics, ethical decision-making, and work-life balance, stoicism has much to offer professionals navigating the complexities of their careers.

As we conclude, it's essential to recognize that embracing stoicism in the workplace isn't a one-time effort, but rather, a continuous process of personal growth and development. The cornerstone of this philosophy lies in our ability to adopt and integrate the principles of stoicism into our everyday professional lives. The impact that stoicism can have on your career is directly proportional to your commitment and willingness to apply its teachings in all aspects of work life.

Making stoicism a constant part of your mindset will provide you with the tools and fortitude necessary to face unexpected challenges, move past setbacks, and create opportunities for personal and professional growth. Moreover, by embracing stoic principles, you will not only benefit yourself but also positively affect those around you, be it colleagues, team members, or the organization as a whole.

Moreover, remember that stoicism isn't a rigid, prescriptive philosophy—it encourages adaptability and continuous self-improvement. As you progress in your career, take the time to reassess and re-align your approach, ensuring that the principles of stoicism remain relevant and effective in driving your growth and job satisfaction.

"Unwavering Success" was written with the intention of sparking your curiosity and enthusiasm for the boundless potential of stoic philosophy in the workplace. As you move forward, bring this knowledge with you, and strive to become an inspiring example for others to follow. Share your newfound insights with your colleagues, contribute to the development of a stoic workplace culture, and take pride in driving the transformation of your professional environment.

Above all, as you embark on this new chapter in your work life, remember that the journey to unwavering success is not a linear path; it is filled with twists and turns. Embrace stoicism as a guide to navigating these complexities with unwavering focus, tenacity, and wisdom. We hope that the insights and teachings garnered from this book will serve as a steadfast companion, empowering you to discover your inner resilience and strength, foster harmonious relationships in the workplace, and forge a fulfilling, balanced life that is deeply rooted in the timeless wisdom of stoicism.

As you make your way through the dynamic landscape of professional life, may the lessons of Unwavering Success serve as shining beacons illuminating your journey towards mastery and joy in work, leadership, and beyond.